EGYPT

Written by

Steve and Patricia Harrison

Illustrated by
John Shackell

Designed by
Bernie Cavender

Edited by
Lisa Hyde

Picture research by
Frances Abraham

Contents

The march of time

▶ 3100 BC   THE ARCHAIC PERIOD

KING MENES
THE FIRST RULER OF ALL EGYPT

WRITING AND METALWORKING DEVELOP

▶ 2700 BC   THE OLD KINGDOM

THE AGE OF THE PYRAMIDS

▶ 2040 BC   THE MIDDLE KINGDOM   CONQUEST OF NUBIA   HORSE-DRAWN CHARIOT INTRODUC

MENTUHOTEP UNITES EGYPT

▶ 1070 BC   THE LATE PERIOD   NUBIANS CONQUER EGYPT   ▶ 663 BC   EGYPT CONQUERED BY TH

EGYPT IN DECLINE · CIVIL WAR

▶ 30 BC

EGYPT BECOMES PART OF THE ROMAN EMPIRE

▶ 45 AD

CHRISTIANITY INTRODUCED IN EGYPT

▶ 300 AD   CHRISTIANS PERSECUTED

COPTIC CHRISTIANITY BEG

▶ 1000 AD

CRUSADERS BATTLE NEAR CAIRO

MAMELUKE DYNASTY

▶ 1517 AD

OTTOMAN TURKS BEGIN LONG RULE OF EG

TRADE GROWS   AGRICULTURE IMPROVES   ▶ 2200 BC   EGYPT DIVIDED

THE SPHINX IS BUILT

PERIOD OF WAR · COLLAPSE OF CENTRAL GOVERNMENT

1570 BC   THE NEW KINGDOM   EGYPT DEFEATS THE SEA PEOPLES   WEAK GOVERNMENT

GREAT WEALTH AND SPLENDOUR

WEAK GOVERNMENT

EGYPT DIVIDED UNDER DIFFERENT RULERS

NS ▶ 525 BC   EGYPT CONQUERED BY THE PERSIANS   ▶ 332 BC   ▶ 48–30 BC

ALEXANDER THE GREAT CONQUERS EGYPT

CLEOPATRA VII
THE LAST GREEK RULER

640 AD   ▶ 820 AD   ▶ 969 AD   CAIRO FOUNDED

THE ARAB ARMIES CONQUER EGYPT

ISLAM INTRODUCED

WAR BETWEEN ARABS AND COPTS MOST COPTS CONVERT TO ISLAM

1798 AD   ▶ 1805 AD   ▶ 1869 AD   ▶ 1953 AD   ▶ 1970→

NAPOLEON INVADES EGYPT

MOHAMMAD ALI TAKES CONTROL AND EGYPT IS MODERNISED

SUEZ CANAL OPENS

BRITISH INFLUENCE STRONG

RED SEA

EGYPT INDEPENDENT RULED BY **PRESIDENT NASSER**

RISING POPULATION

OVER 50 MILLION

INCREASED FOOD PRODUCTION

Digging for the past

We can learn about the past in a variety of ways. Photographs, paintings, books, writing, talking and objects provide us with evidence. We use different sources of evidence in order to build up an overall picture of the past. One important consideration for all who want to learn more about the past is that we must *preserve* as much evidence as possible. This has not always been the case.

Thieves have always been ready to steal ancient treasures and either sell them or melt them down into precious metals. Many great treasures were lost to grave-robbers over the centuries.

During the nineteenth century Europeans visited Egypt in order to find ancient objects and send them to their own countries.

Belzoni

One of the most famous European adventurers in Egypt was an Italian called Giovanni Belzoni.

He was over two metres tall and worked as a fairground strongman in England before travelling to Egypt to sell machinery.

Once there he realised that sending objects to Europe could make him rich. He is remembered for moving the giant head of Ramesses II across the desert to the Nile from where it could be shipped to England. It still stands in the British Museum today.

Belzoni was asked:
'Have you a scarcity of stones also in Europe, that you come here to take them away?'

He answered:
'We have plenty of stones but we think these in Egypt are of a better sort.'

Modern archaeologists working in Egypt record exactly what they find and where they find it. Objects are removed from the ground with great care and are then treated so that they can be preserved.

In the picture above you can see an archaeologist at work at the Temple of Hatshepsut in the Valley of Luxor. For more on this Pharaoh see page 14.

The day of days

Howard Carter was searching for an undiscovered tomb of a Pharaoh. His work was paid for by Lord Carnarvon, who announced that this was the last year he could afford to support the search.

1 NOVEMBER 1922
I enrolled my workmen and was ready to begin.

4 NOVEMBER 1922
Something out of the ordinary happened. A step cut in the rock had been discovered.

25 NOVEMBER 1922
We unblocked the door and found a descending passage filled with stone and rubble.

26 NOVEMBER 1922
The day of days. We came upon a second sealed doorway.

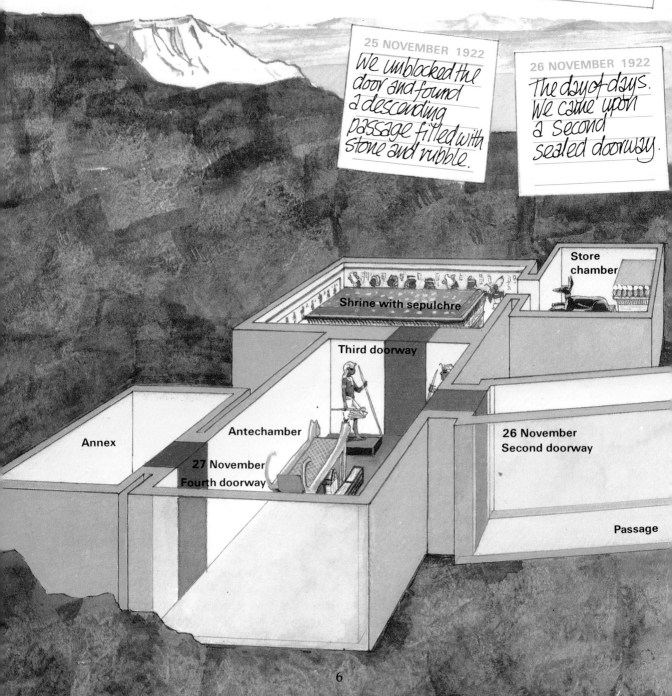

Store chamber

Shrine with sepulchre

Third doorway

Annex

Antechamber

27 November
Fourth doorway

26 November
Second doorway

Passage

5 NOVEMBER 1922

Step succeeded step; towards sunset, there was disclosed the upper part of a doorway

6 NOVEMBER 1922

Cable to Lord Carnarvon in England: "A magnificent tomb with seals intact."

23 NOVEMBER 1922

Lord Carnarvon arrives.

24 NOVEMBER 1922

The whole staircase was clear. We made out the name of Tutankhamun.

27 NOVEMBER 1922

Careful inspection of the Antechamber and discovery of the Annex.

29 NOVEMBER 1922

Official opening.

3 DECEMBER 1922

Tomb sealed against thieves.

25 DECEMBER 1922

The first object was removed from the tomb.

4 November Entrance

Staircase

5 November First doorway

November

'With trembling hands I made a tiny breach in the upper left hand corner . . . widening the hole a little I inserted the candle and peered in . . . at first I could see nothing, the hot air escaping from the chamber causing the candle flame to flicker, presently details of the room emerged slowly from the mist, strange animals, statues and gold – everywhere the glint of gold.'

Tutankhamun revealed

Thieves had raided the ante-chamber soon after the burial. They had taken only small, valuable, easily-carried objects. Other larger items had been thrown around the chamber and were piled up in heaps when Carter first saw them.

There were more than 2,000 separate objects in the four rooms of the tomb. Many were covered in gold. Carter had photographs taken before they began to remove the objects from the tomb.

Carter described what he saw: '. . . exquisitely painted and inlaid caskets; alabaster vases; bouquets of flowers or leaves; beds; chairs beautifully carved; a golden inlaid throne; a heap of curious white oviform boxes; on the left a confused pile of overturned chariots, glistening with gold and inlay.'

Carter began work on the coffins of Tutankhamun in October. There was a wooden outer coffin, a second coffin covered in gold and a third coffin made of *solid* gold. Inside this coffin lay the body of the Pharaoh, the head and shoulders covered with what Carter called 'a brilliant, magnificent, burnished gold mask'.

Activity
● How many of the objects can you see in the photographs?

The death mask of Tutankhamun

Man or god?

Tutankhamun is the only Pharaoh who has been discovered in the wrapping, coffins and sarcophagus in which he was buried. It was decided to examine the body in the tomb.

Investigation results

Head:	clean shaven
Eyelashes:	very long
Earlobes:	perforated by circular hole 7.5 mm in diameter
Skull	empty
Teeth:	wisdom teeth partly developed
Height:	1.676 metres (5 feet 6 inches)
Age:	about 18 (evidence of bone development)

Most of the treasures found in the tomb are now in the Cairo Museum. The body has been reburied in the tomb.

The whole world remembers Tutankhamun because of the marvellous treasures discovered in his tomb. We should remember, however, that he was only young when he died. Many other Pharaohs were far more powerful than he was. We can only imagine what *their* tombs must have contained. As Howard Carter said, 'If they could bury this unimportant king with so much splendour, whatever must the tomb of a well-established Pharaoh have looked like?'

Activity
● List the arguments for and against the unwrapping and examination of the body of Tutankhamun.

Headdress
The vulture symbolised power over Upper Egypt, the cobra power over Lower Egypt.

Crook
The Pharaoh was the shepherd of all his people. The crook is also a symbol of Osiris.

Flail
A symbol of the god Osiris.

False beard
A symbol to show the Pharaoh is a god.

The Crowns of Egypt

The Blue War Crown

The White Crown of Upper Egypt

The Red Crown of the Delta Region

The Double Crown was worn by the ruler of all Egypt

Jewellery
Includes the scarab – symbol of the sun-god, giver of life.

Buckle
The name of the Pharaoh was engraved on the belt buckle.

Sandals
Gold was used for the thong. Gold toe covers were also used on mummies.

The power of the Pharaohs

The Pharaoh was the most important person in Egypt. He was in charge of the army, the navy, the law courts, religion and the government. He owned all the land, the property and the wealth of Egypt. Occasionally the Pharaoh was a Queen and not a King.

Rulership

Pharaohs ruled Egypt through a large number of officials. It is possible to think of Ancient Egypt as organised like a pyramid.

At the base were the poorest people – servants, labourers and peasants. Above them were the craftsmen – skilled workers like stonemasons, carpenters, potters, jewellers and smiths.

Next would be the officials who carried out the day-to-day running of the country. Also in this class were the scribes and minor priests.

Just below the Pharaoh were the people with real power – high priests and priestesses, nobles and chief government officials. Many of these people were related to the Pharaoh.

In order to show how powerful they were the Pharaohs built fine palaces and magnificent statues. They carried out daily religious rituals when they acted as gods and were seen as god-kings by the people.

Ramesses II is remembered for the buildings and monuments during his 67 years as Pharaoh. He was a warlike Pharaoh who fought the Hittites. He was also the father of more than one hundred children!

The temple of Hatshepsut

Hatshepsut's temple at Deir el Bahri has been described as 'the finest building in Egypt' and 'one of the great buildings of the world'.

Hatshepsut was a remarkable woman. A daughter of Pharaoh Tuthmosis I, she married her half-brother Tuthmosis II. They had no children but Tuthmosis had a secondary wife who gave birth to a son. When Tuthmosis II died Hatshepsut decided she would rule rather than allow the son of her husband and his secondary wife to become Pharaoh. She declared herself Pharaoh and ruled for twenty years. She wore a false beard, appeared like a typical male Pharaoh and was more than a match for her enemies.

Most priests did not stay in the temple all year. Many would live with their families for nine months of the year. Priests had to lead simple lives. They shaved their heads and bodies every three days. They wore plain white linen and sandals. They had a special diet and bathed three times a day. As the temple was a god's house the main duty was to look after the god.

There were different kinds of temple. Most were built as homes for the gods and in such temples a strict daily routine had to be followed.

Each day the statue of the god was cleaned, its clothes changed and offerings of food and drink were made.

The god was woken each morning by a group of priests who sang and danced.

Many temples had schools attached. The priests were educated and in turn they provided education for others.

Tombs for eternity

When most people think of Egypt they think of the magnificent pyramids built by the Pharaohs. Pyramids are not all like the great pyramids at Giza shown in the photograph.

The first pyramids looked like large benches and were called 'mastabas', the Arabic word for bench. At first these were made from brick. As the Pharaohs and other nobles became richer the mastabas they built became larger, often containing many rooms for storing the possessions which would be needed in the next life.

King Zoser planned to be buried in a mastaba but his chief minister, Imhotep, suggested that Zoser should construct a much finer building, one which went up in steps rather like a number of mastabas one above the other. King Zoser's tomb was the first **Step Pyramid**.

Mastaba

Step Pyramid

A later development was to 'fill in' the steps with granite or limestone slabs which gave the pyramids smooth sides. This type is known as a **True Pyramid**.

The pyramid builders

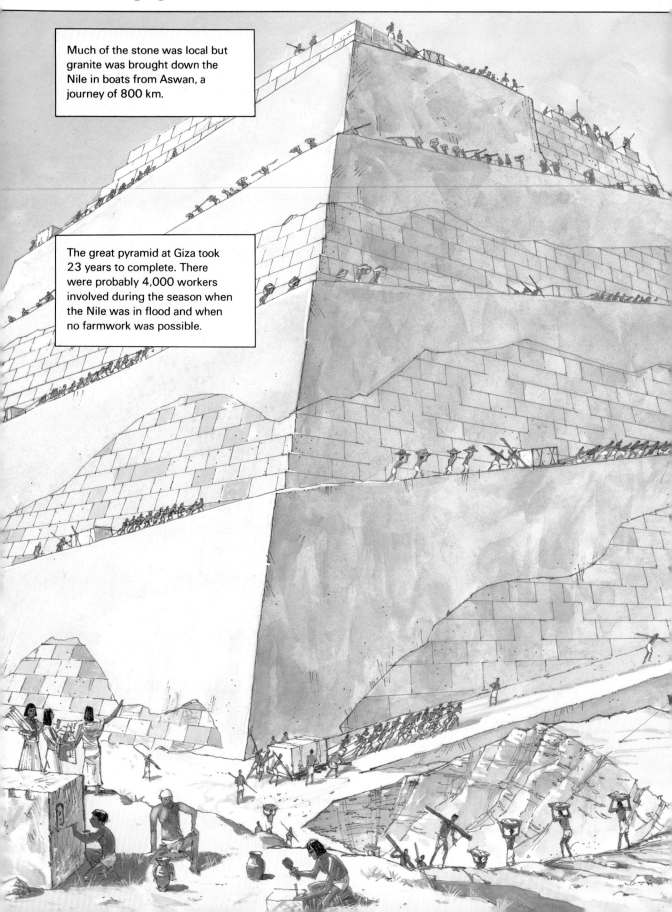

Much of the stone was local but granite was brought down the Nile in boats from Aswan, a journey of 800 km.

The great pyramid at Giza took 23 years to complete. There were probably 4,000 workers involved during the season when the Nile was in flood and when no farmwork was possible.

Ramps were built along the four sides of the pyramid. A ramp ran from each of the corners. Three were used for going up, one for going down.

People worked in teams. Each large stone block had a quarry mark painted on it. Some of these marks gave a team name – 'the vigorous gang' – or even funny comments like 'the king is drunk'.

The Egyptian stonemasons could cut the limestone with their copper chisels, but copper was not hard enough to cut granite. Special hammers were used to make slots and wood was hammered into the slots. The wood was soaked, so it expanded and split the granite.

Decay: solving the problem

Ginger

If you visit the British Museum in London and ask to see 'Ginger', you will be shown a man who lived more than 5,000 years ago. He was an Egyptian who died about 3200 BC. In those days fertile land was not used for burials as it would have been a waste of good land. Ginger's body was wrapped in matting and taken to the hot, dry desert where it was buried in a shallow grave.

Dead bodies rot when bacteria get to work. Bacteria need moisture to develop but Ginger's body had no moisture, as the hot sand had soaked it all up.

Therefore Ginger's body did not decay.

You can see from the photograph that Ginger was buried along with knives and pots which would have contained food and drink. This *evidence* tells us that the people who buried him expected Ginger to carry on living in some way. The objects were there to help him in his next life.

The Egyptians believed that the body needed to be preserved so that after death the spirit would be able to recognise the body and give it continued life.

Methods of burial

Wealthy people wanted to be buried differently. They were unhappy at just being put into the desert sand. They also wanted to take valuable objects with them to the next life. Specially built underground chambers were made from wood, brick or stone. The sand was kept out and the chambers were often damp. They had not realised how important the hot, dry sand was for preserving bodies.

The Egyptians had to find ways of stopping the body from rotting away if the bodies of the rich and powerful were to enter the next life. Sand would work but it left the skin very tight and the body did not look very lifelike. They needed something which would remove moisture but leave the body looking more like it did when alive. The solution was **Natron**, a salty substance which was found around the sides of lakes near Cairo.

The word **mummy** has nothing to do with Mother. Sometimes, when the mummification was done badly, the body turned darker and became very brittle. Bits would break off easily. People thought the bodies looked like bitumen (similar to tar). The Arabic word for bitumen is 'mummiya', and that is how the mummy got its name.

The ritual of embalming

It was important to begin work on the body as soon as possible after death. The body would be taken to the banks of the Nile and given a ritual washing.

This washing was a sign of the rebirth of the dead person. The body was then taken to a tent or building where the embalming began.

The brain was removed, usually down the nostril, and thrown away. A cut was made in the stomach and the insides removed. The heart, however, was left in the body.

The parts of the body removed were dried in Natron. They were cleaned, perfumed and wrapped in cloth. They were then put into four canopic jars and the jars placed in a wooden chest which was buried with the mummy.

The empty body was rinsed out and then packed full of temporary stuffing which helped to speed up the drying out. All sorts of materials were used, from rags and sand to dry grass. The stuffed body was covered with Natron.

The table was at an angle so as liquid drained out of the body it would soak away. The Natron was left in place for 40 days. Many bodies would be in the embalmer's building at the same time and the smell would have been awful!

The stuffing was removed but not thrown away. It now contained bits of the dead person and so might be needed in the next world. The body was now washed, dried and stuffed again. This meant the body kept some of its original shape.

The skin was shrivelled because of the Natron and needed to be softened with lotions. The cut in the stomach was stitched or sealed. The body was coated with resin to make it firm and waterproof. Then the body was bandaged – a ritual which lasted 15 days.

In early times the bandaged body was placed in a wooden coffin. Later the wealthy had a mummy mask made. A face was painted on and a wig attached. Royal bodies had golden masks. A later development was the use of a whole-body cover.

This was in two parts and the body lay in the base and a lid was placed over it. It was the full length and shape of the body. Many of these coffins were highly decorated.

This life and the next

One final ceremony had to be performed before the mummy was placed in the coffin. This ceremony was known as 'The Opening of the Mouth'. The mummy was held up by a priest dressed as the god Anubis. A second priest, who acted as the dead person's son, touched the mummy's mouth with an *adze*. They believed that *ba*, the breath, would enter the mummy and give it new life. The ceremony gave back to the mummy all its senses which were lost at death.

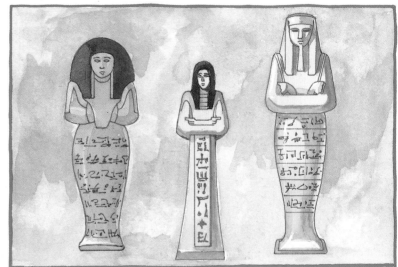

All Egyptians hoped to enter paradise – 'The Fields of Yaru' – where the land was rich and plentiful. Even in paradise work had to be done in the fields and on the canals. Egyptians made sure 'shabtis' (small statues) were placed in their tombs with them. These shabtis carried tools and did all the hard work in the next world, leaving the dead free to enjoy their new life.

Judgement

The dead had a kind of guidebook to help them on their journey to a new life in paradise. This was called the 'Book of the Dead'. It told of what they must do to reach paradise.

Firstly they had to be judged. The god Osiris and 42 judges listened to the dead, who would claim they had done nothing wrong during their lives – no murder, no cheating, no rustling. In fact, no evil at all.

Next the dead person's heart was weighed. On one side of the balance was a feather, the symbol of truth. The heart was placed on the opposite side. If the two pans stayed in balance then the heart was truthful and the dead person could enter the land of Osiris, paradise. If the heart was heavier than the feather the person was a liar and would be eaten by the devourer, a beast who waited below the scales, ready to pounce!

Those who passed the test were met by Horus, the falcon-headed god, and taken to the Fields of Yaru.

Gods: great and small

In early times the Egyptians worshipped gods of the natural world – gods of sun, rain, rivers and the wind. They also worshipped animal gods. As time passed belief in many of these gods changed. They became more like human beings but still with animal parts.

Each large city and area had its own god. Only a few gods became national gods, worshipped in all Egypt. They were important to the rich and powerful and great temples were built in their honour. Ordinary people probably spent more time praying to their local god, sometimes even a family, household god.

Rich and poor worshipped together at national festival times. They danced and sang in celebration.

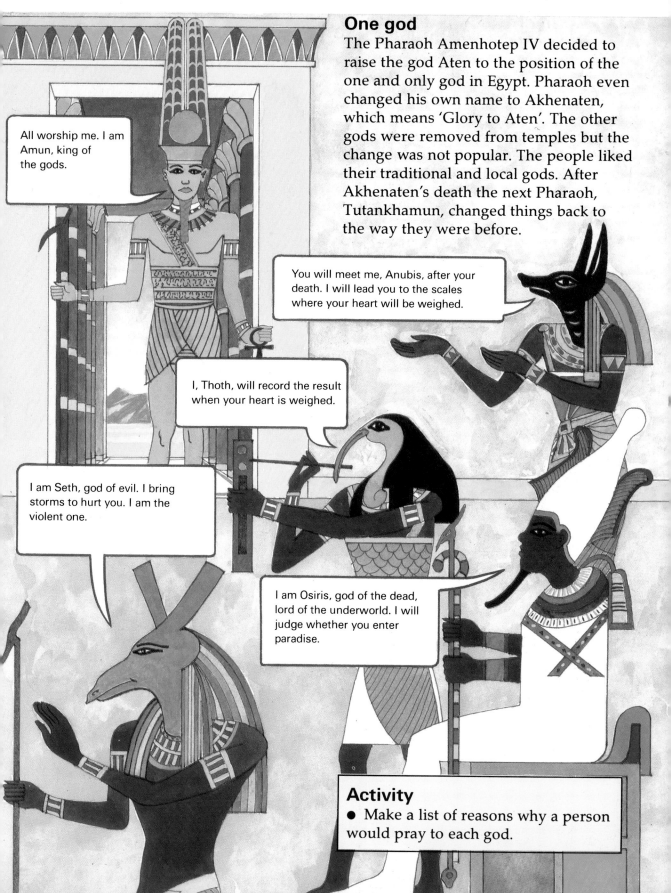

One god

The Pharaoh Amenhotep IV decided to raise the god Aten to the position of the one and only god in Egypt. Pharaoh even changed his own name to Akhenaten, which means 'Glory to Aten'. The other gods were removed from temples but the change was not popular. The people liked their traditional and local gods. After Akhenaten's death the next Pharaoh, Tutankhamun, changed things back to the way they were before.

Activity
● Make a list of reasons why a person would pray to each god.

Myths and legends

Day and night

People long ago did not have the knowledge about the world that we have. They tried to explain everyday events as the actions of the gods.

We know the Nile flooded because of melting snow and heavy rain far to the south. They explained it as the action of the god called Hapi. We know that darkness and light happen as the earth revolves. When our area faces the sun it is daytime, and when it faces away we have the darkness of night.

The Egyptians had their own explanation for night and day. They told of Geb the earth god and of his wife Nut the day goddess. Between them stood Shu, the god of the atmosphere who held Nut in place. As the sun set in the evening the Egyptians believed it had been swallowed by Nut. Through the dark night the sun remained in Nut's body, hidden from view. At the end of the night the sun was born again from Nut and brought a new day's light to the world.

Osiris

Osiris was a great god-king. During his reign the people were happy and well-fed. Osiris' brother Seth was jealous of the king's success.

Seth invited Osiris to a feast, captured him, locked him in a chest and threw him in the river.

Osiris' wife Isis searched and found the chest and returned it to Egypt from Phoenicia.

This time Seth was determined not to have Osiris back. He cut his body into fourteen pieces and had them scattered far and wide.

Isis did not give up. She found the parts of the body and put them back together.

She then asked Anubis and Nephthys to help her. They produced the first mummy.

Isis brought up her baby, Horus, in secret. She was afraid Seth would find and murder him.

When he was fully grown Horus challenged Seth and a terrible fight took place.

The gods decided Horus should be king. He took on the powers of Osiris who then became king of paradise.

Eternal life

Egyptians, like other farming people, knew that plants grow, die and grow again in the next season. They believed that what happens to plants could also happen to people and to the gods. The myth of Osiris was the story of the god who died to be born again.

Communicating from the past

One reason we know a great deal about the Egyptians is because they wrote so much. We have examples of their writing dating back more than 5,000 years. Their earliest form of writing is called *hieroglyphic* (writing using pictures). This type of writing was used on great monuments in Egypt for over 3,000 years.

Each picture-sign meant the object it showed, so wwww meant *water*. The same picture-sign could also mean a sound. wwww stands for *n*.

There were over 700 hieroglyphs, so anyone who wanted to become a scribe would have to learn them all! Hieroglyphic script took a long time to write, so easier, shortened versions were developed.

Activities

● A few of the hieroglyphs are shown in the table next to the nearest sound from our modern alphabet.
● Can you decode the hieroglyphs at the top of these pages?
● Read the message on the scroll. Where should it be displayed?
● Write a message using hieroglyphs.

30

Hieratic and Demotic script

Hieratic developed first and was used in business writing. **Demotic** came later, and was used for everyday writing by educated people and remained in use until 1,500 years ago. Hieratic and Demotic scripts were usually written on **papyrus** (paper).

Translation

Translating hieroglyphs seems easy when we have a chart to help us but it took 20 years of hard work by a Frenchman, Jean-François Champollion, before the modern world could understand the writings of ancient Egypt.

At the beginning of the nineteenth century no one knew how to translate the hieroglyphs. Their meaning was a mystery.

The clue to solving the mystery was a black stone found by a French soldier at Rosetta in 1799. This stone contained three texts, Hieroglyphic, Demotic and Greek. By comparing the three texts Champollion was eventually able to crack the code.

Some words in the text were written in a sort of bracket, called a cartouche. Champollion recognised the name PTOLEMYS in a cartouche in the Greek text. He guessed that the cartouches in the other texts would say the same. He was right! It took many more years to work out what every hieroglyph meant, but Champollion's work had made it possible.

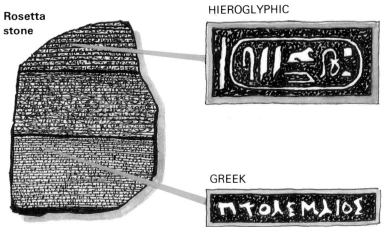

Rosetta stone

HIEROGLYPHIC

GREEK

Papyrus making

Papyrus reeds grew in the marshes along the Nile. These were cut down and taken to workshops. The reeds were cut into short lengths, peeled and the inside pith sliced into thin strips. The strips were placed side by side in two layers – one vertical and one horizontal. Cloth was placed over them and they were pressed together. The natural juices in the papyrus acted as a glue. The paper was ready after being polished with a stone.

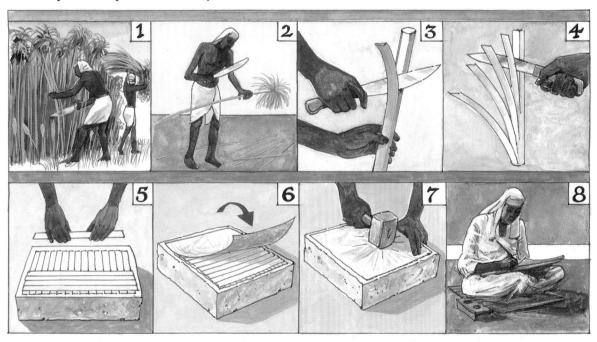

Time for work

The palaces, pyramids and temples of Ancient Egypt could only have been built in a rich country. The wealth of Egypt was based on agriculture. The food produced fed the population, and taxes on agriculture paid for the nobles' high standard of living.

Workers specialised in different jobs. We can learn about the way they worked from the evidence of wall paintings and papyrus.

Harvesting wheat

The wheat is first cut and carried in baskets to be raked. The wheat is then trodden on by oxen. Winnowing follows, when the chaff blows away leaving only the grain.

A scribe would check the amount, while other scribes would record it. Tax was calculated on the amount of land farmed. Those who did not pay were beaten.

Wine-making

The grapes were picked with great care. They were placed into a large press and the workers would tread them so that the juice flowed out. It was poured into jars to ferment. Later the jars were sealed. Just like today wine was labelled, providing information about the grower, the date of production and the type of wine. The tax gatherer used this information.

Crafts

Craftwork was specialised. Skills were handed down from father to son.

Carpenters used techniques similar to those used today. Metalworkers had every piece of raw metal weighed before they were given it. Metals were very expensive in Ancient Egypt and many workers could not be trusted.

Brick makers

Homes and ordinary buildings were made of clay bricks. The wet clay was shaped into brick form, placed in the hot sun to bake and then used for building.

Time for play

There is a great deal of evidence about how the Egyptians relaxed and enjoyed life.

The banquet

The nobles held great banquets. Men and women sometimes sat apart, at opposite sides of the room. The guests were served large quantities of wine and beer. They ate oxen, pigeon, fowl and a wide variety of cakes, biscuits and bread. Sometimes guests had too much and were sick.

There would be dancing provided by young women who performed movements which included gymnastics, as well as chorus-girl dancing.

Music

There are many pictures of blind musicians. The Egyptians did not have a written system for their music. In the Old Kingdom most musicians were men, but during the New Kingdom it seems that women musicians were more common. String and wind instruments were played, as were drums and tambourines.

Games

Adults and children enjoyed a variety of games. Ball games, spinning tops, toy animals, dolls and marbles were all used by children. Their parents played board games, read stories and listened to professional story-tellers.

Hunting

One of the favourite pastimes of the rich was hunting.

Some hunted animals with bows and arrows. Others fished or attempted to hit fowl with a special stick shaped like a snake, which the noble would throw at the bird.

Bridge across time

The power of the Pharaohs gradually declined. Egypt was often controlled by foreign powers.

In 332 BC Alexander the Great of Macedonia (Greece) conquered Egypt. When he died one of his generals, Ptolemy, took control. Ptolemy and his descendants ruled for 300 years. The Ptolemies were Greek speakers but they acted like Pharaohs and allowed the Egyptians to keep their customs.

Cleopatra was the last of the Greeks. She ruled Egypt for 21 years but needed Roman support. The Roman Empire was divided by civil war. Cleopatra's Roman husband, Mark Antony, was defeated in battle by Octavian. Cleopatra committed suicide by holding a poisonous asp to her breast. The last Greek ruler was dead, and Egypt would be part of the Roman Empire for the next 700 years.

Under this rule the people of Egypt became Christians, but they were unhappy with their foreign rulers who seemed to exploit Egypt for the benefit of their capital city of Byzantium.

A new power emerged in 622 AD when the Prophet Muhammad began to spread the word of **Islam**. Soon Arab armies won victories throughout North Africa and the Middle East. In 642 AD an Arab Muslim army defeated the Byzantines in Egypt.

Different Muslim dynasties have ruled Egypt since then. Magnificent art and architecture were produced – the finest since the Pharaohs. Medicine, geography, mathematics and literature were of a very high quality. When the Christian armies of Europe invaded during the crusades they were defeated and Egypt remained Muslim. From 1517 AD the Muslim rulers were Turkish and many Egyptians resented this.

In 1798 Egypt was invaded by a French army led by Napoleon. He believed it would help his plans for moving against India and would badly affect British power. The British, Turks and French fought a number of battles. The French were defeated and left Egypt. A young soldier who fought the French, Muhammad Ali, later led the Egyptians in battle against Turkish rule. He became ruler of Egypt and his descendants were heads of state until 1952.

The Suez Canal was opened in 1869. It shortened the route from Europe to India and the Far East.

Bad rule led to the involvement of France and Britain in controlling

Egyptian government. This was resented by many Egyptians and fighting broke out in 1882. The British invaded and ran the country until 1936, when Egypt was recognised as an independent nation. British and German armies fought each other there during the Second World War.

The Egyptians objected to Britain still having influence in their country – particularly along the Suez Canal.

In 1952 the army removed the Egyptian king, Faruq, and Egypt became a republic. The new leader was Colonel Nasser. In 1956 Britain, France and Israel invaded Egypt in order to control the Suez Canal. The rest of the world objected. The foreign armies withdrew and President Nasser became a great Egyptian hero.

In recent years wars have been fought with Israel.

President Nasser died in 1970. He was succeeded by President Sadat, who was assassinated in 1981. President Mubarak became President in the same year.

The gift of the Nile

There is little rainfall in Egypt. The water the country needs is provided by one of the world's greatest rivers – the Nile.

In summer the snow melts on the mountains of Ethiopia and Central Africa and the rain falls. An enormous volume of water begins to flow along the White Nile and the Blue Nile. The two rivers join together near Khartoum and the floodwater continues its journey north to Egypt.

For thousands of years the Nile flooded its banks in Egypt in July and August. Rich silt was deposited on the valley edge leaving the land very fertile and ready for cultivation. The crops grew in the spring and were harvested before the next flood.

The great buildings were all constructed on land close to the Nile, but not close enough to be flooded. Fertile land was too precious to build on.

In Ancient Egypt stone barrages were built to divert the water onto the fields and into large 'tanks'. These were rather like basins surrounded by clay edges. In this way water could be retained longer, helping more crops to grow.

In 1971 a great dam was finished at Aswan. The dam makes it possible to control the flow of water so it does not simply arrive in one flood period. A regular supply of water along canals means more than one crop a year can be grown.

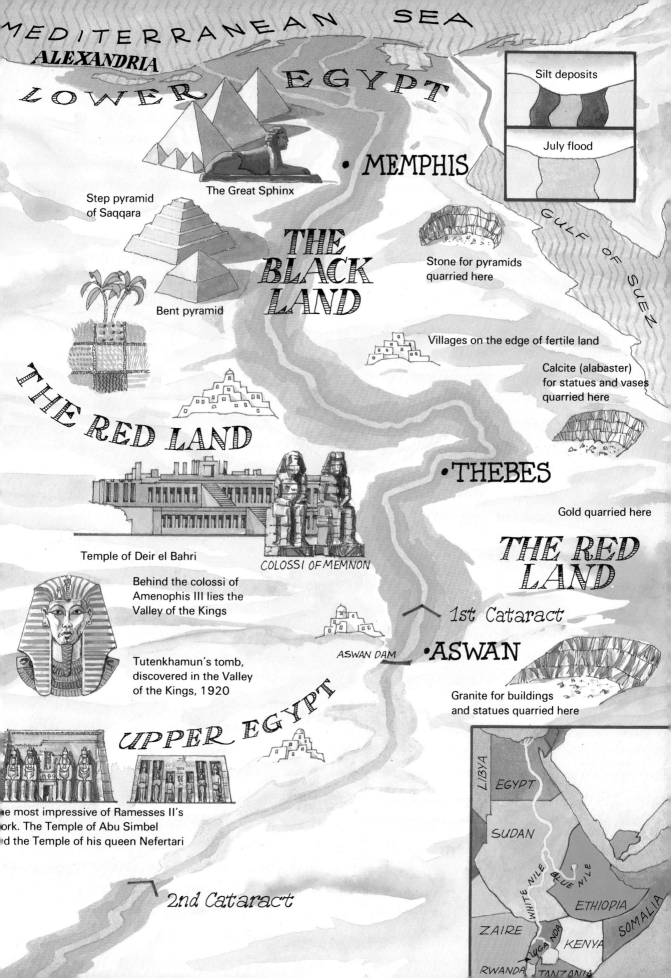

MEDITERRANEAN SEA

ALEXANDRIA

LOWER EGYPT

Silt deposits

July flood

The Great Sphinx

•MEMPHIS

GULF OF SUEZ

THE BLACK LAND

Step pyramid of Saqqara

Stone for pyramids quarried here

Bent pyramid

Villages on the edge of fertile land

THE RED LAND

Calcite (alabaster) for statues and vases quarried here

Temple of Deir el Bahri

COLOSSI OF MEMNON

•THEBES

Gold quarried here

THE RED LAND

Behind the colossi of Amenophis III lies the Valley of the Kings

1st Cataract

ASWAN DAM

•ASWAN

Tutenkhamun's tomb, discovered in the Valley of the Kings, 1920

Granite for buildings and statues quarried here

UPPER EGYPT

...e most impressive of Ramesses II's ...ork. The Temple of Abu Simbel ...d the Temple of his queen Nefertari

2nd Cataract

LIBYA

EGYPT

SUDAN

WHITE NILE BLUE NILE

ETHIOPIA

ZAIRE

KENYA SOMALIA

RWANDA TANZANIA

Living faiths

The vast majority of Egyptians are Muslims. The Islamic world has two main groups – Sunni and Shi'a Muslims. In Egypt most Muslims are Sunni.

Islam teaches that there is only one God (Allah) and that Muhammed was the last of his prophets. The Holy Book of Islam is the Qur'an.

Muslims should pray five times a day. Often the prayer takes place in the *mosque*. Egypt has many magnificent mosques. The Al-Azhar mosque in Cairo has one of the world's oldest universities attached to it. Muslim students from all over the world come here to study.

There are countless small mosques providing local places of worship throughout the cities and in the villages.

One of the first things a European visitor notices is the 'Call to Prayer' which is heard five times a day. A muezzin climbs the minaret above the mosque and calls on the faithful to prepare for prayer. In modern Egypt it is often a tape recording broadcast by loudspeaker, but the effect is the same.

Islam

There are arguments in Egypt today about what being a Muslim means. Some people believe that modern influences and contact with the West are un-Islamic. Sometimes riots take place, and theatres and nightclubs are attacked.

President Sadat was assassinated by Muslims who were unhappy with his leadership.

Occasionally there is trouble between Muslims and the other main religious group – the Copts.

Coptic Christianity

There is a belief that Christianity was brought to Egypt by St Mark. Those Egyptians who did not speak Greek followed a type of Christianity named after their language – Coptic.

Most of Egypt followed the Coptic faith up to the time of the Muslim invasions. The conquerors were tolerant of the Copts and the religion has continued into modern times. It is impossible to say how many Egyptians are Christian, but it is probably about 10 per cent of the population.

Coptic churches are found in many parts of Egypt. Alexandria is the centre of the faith. The leader of the Copts – the Patriarch – is based there.

Cairo, mother of the world

Cairo is a noisy, crowded, busy and lively city. It is the largest city in Africa and most visitors find it an exciting place to be. Magnificent ancient mosques stand close to the modern skyscrapers. Donkey carts queue alongside Mercedes cars in the daily traffic jams. The languages of Africa, the Middle East and Europe can be heard in the pavement cafés. Wherever you turn there are people – young and old, rich and poor, men, women and children – and the number is increasing every year.

No one is quite sure how many people live in Cairo, but it is probably more than 12 million. Large numbers of Cairenes need to travel around on public transport. The buses are sometimes crowded to bursting point, but the brand-new underground system is cheap and clean and runs on time.

Cairo: an historic city

The ancient capital of the Old Kingdom of the Pharaohs was at Memphis, 20 km south of Cairo. Other settlements existed in the Cairo area but it was only when the Arab conquerors came to Egypt in the seventh century that Cairo became the chief city of the country. Today visitors can see evidence of the past all around them. One highlight of any visit to Cairo is the Museum of Egyptian Antiquities. There you can see over 100,000 exhibits, including many of the magnificent treasures from the tomb of Tutenkhamun.

The growth of the city has resulted in thousands of hectares of good farmland being used for housing. Egypt needs to produce more and more food for its growing population. The loss of agricultural land makes this more difficult to achieve.

Cairo has many poor people but it does not have the extreme poverty of some large cities. The Government tries to ensure that everyone has enough to eat so there is little or no starvation in Cairo.

Egypt today

The economy of Egypt was badly damaged by the wars against Israel in 1967 and 1973. Great progress has been made since. Today Egypt's income comes from a number of different sources, all of them important to the Egyptian economy. Agriculture remains the largest employer of labour.

New technology has been introduced in some rural areas but there are still many farms which depend on traditional methods of agriculture.

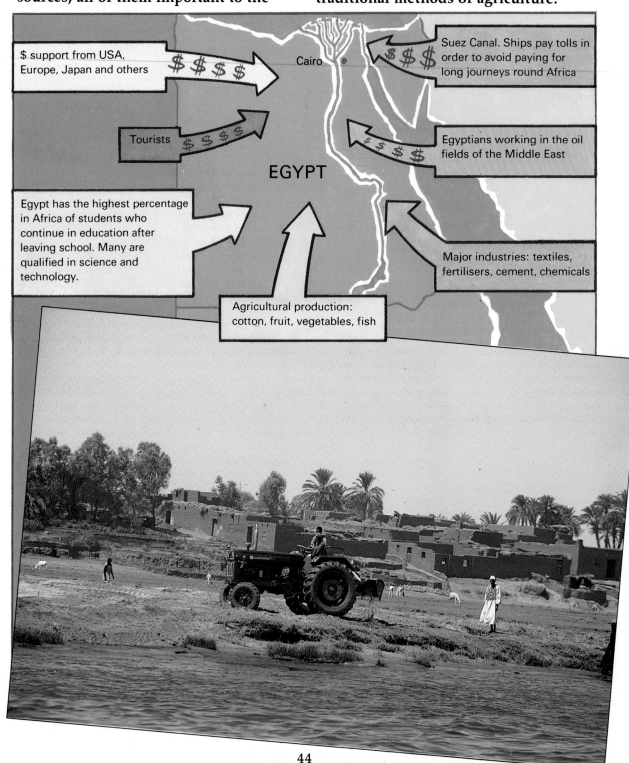

$ support from USA, Europe, Japan and others

Cairo

Suez Canal. Ships pay tolls in order to avoid paying for long journeys round Africa

Tourists

EGYPT

Egyptians working in the oil fields of the Middle East

Egypt has the highest percentage in Africa of students who continue in education after leaving school. Many are qualified in science and technology.

Major industries: textiles, fertilisers, cement, chemicals

Agricultural production: cotton, fruit, vegetables, fish

The building of the Aswan High Dam has had a dramatic effect on the lives of all Egyptians. The dam itself is 3 km wide and 111m high. It holds back the 500 km-long Lake Nasser.

By releasing the water throughout the year it is now possible to grow two and sometimes three crops a year on some land. New land has been irrigated and grows much-needed food to help feed the increasing population.

As the water passes through the dam it drives turbines which provide electricity for Egyptian industry and homes.

There are problems, however. The mud that once brought natural fertilisers to the Nile valley no longer arrives. Artificial fertilisers are used instead. Salt deposits in the soil have increased and year-round water has made it easier for certain waterborne diseases to spread.

Facts and figures

Egypt's population has been rising rapidly since the 1950s. The main factors are improvements in health (fewer babies die), education and food production. The population is increasing by about 1 million a year.

   Most of Egypt is desert. Few people live in the desert regions. More than 95 per cent of Egypt's 50 million population lives in the Nile Delta and along the fertile narrow strip which runs alongside the Nile.

Activities
● Check the positions of Aswan and Alexandria on a map. Why do you think Aswan is so much hotter than Alexandria?
● If you were to visit Egypt, what time of year would you choose? Look carefully at the temperatures before you decide.
● When do you think most tourists visit Egypt?
● In which age groups does Egypt have the largest numbers?
● At what age do most people you know marry and have children?
● Can you predict whether Egypt's population will rise or fall in the next ten years?

Temperature

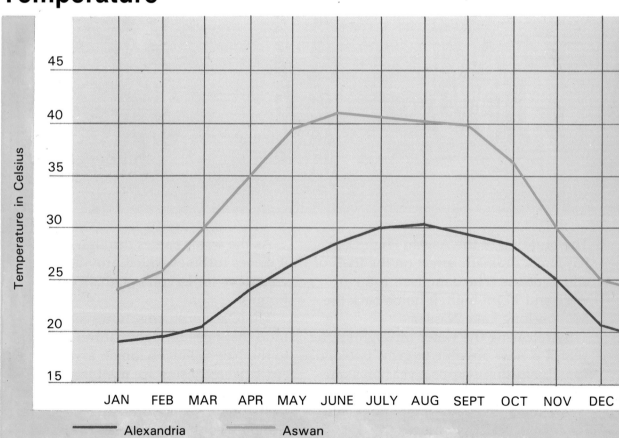

Arabic Numbers

٢	٩	٨	٧	٦	٥	٤	٣	٢	١
10	9	8	7	6	5	4	3	2	1

Population of Egypt

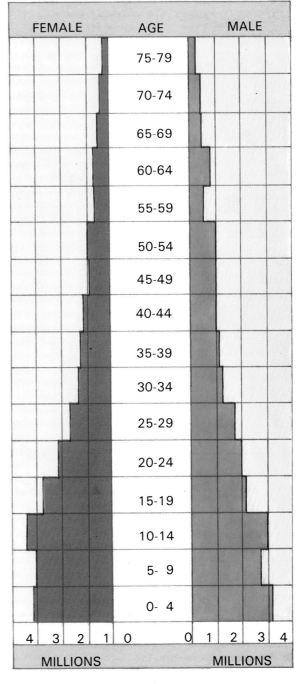

1990

1980

1970

1960

1950

1940

1930

1920

1910

1900

= 10 million people (10,000,000)

FEMALE				AGE	MALE			
				75-79				
				70-74				
				65-69				
				60-64				
				55-59				
				50-54				
				45-49				
				40-44				
				35-39				
				30-34				
				25-29				
				20-24				
				15-19				
				10-14				
				5- 9				
				0- 4				
4	3	2	1	0 0	1	2	3	4
MILLIONS					MILLIONS			

Index ~~~~ 𓃀 𓊨 𓌃 𓏏 𓂋 𓏲 𓅱 𓏭 𓂝

Published by BBC Educational Publishing, a division of BBC Enterprises Limited Woodlands,80 Wood Lane,London,W12 0TT

First published 1990
© Steve and Patricia Harrison/BBC Enterprises Limited 1990
The moral rights of the authors have been asserted
Illustrations © John Shackell

Paperback ISBN 0 563 34589 6
Hardback ISBN 0 563 34754 6

Typeset by Ace Filmsetting Ltd, Frome, Somerset
Text printed and bound in Great Britain by Cambus Litho
Colour reproduction by Dot Gradations Ltd
Cover printed by Richard Clay Ltd

Picture credits

Ancient Art & Architecture Collection **p. 32**; Barnaby's Picture Library **p. 13**; British Museum **front cover** and **pp. 20, 23 & 35**; J. Allan Cash Photolibrary **pp. 5, 38 & 45**; Griffith Institute, Ashmolean Museum **p. 7, 8** *all* & **10**; Robert Harding Picture Library **pp. 4** (© British Museum), **9 & 44**; Mansell Collection **pp. 36–7** *main picture*; Popperfoto **p. 37** *inset*; Spectrum Colour Library **pp. 42–3**; Zefa Picture Library **pp. 14–15 & 16–17**.